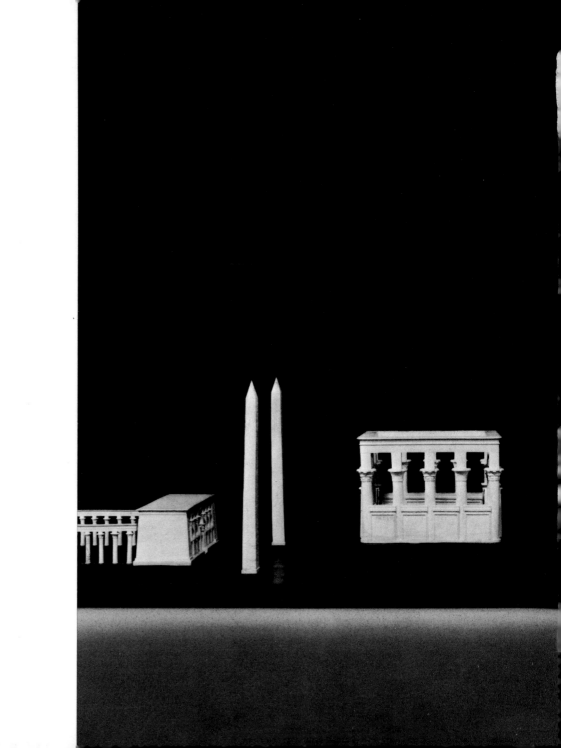

THE SÈVRES EGYPTIAN SERVICE 1810 – 12

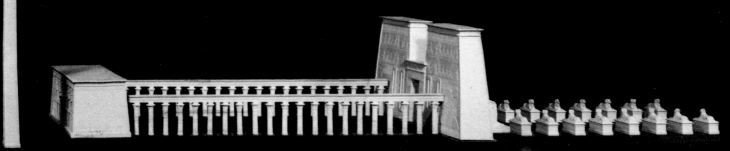

CHARLES TRUMAN, DEPARTMENT OF CERAMICS

VICTORIA AND ALBERT MUSEUM

ACKNOWLEDGEMENTS

I should like to express my thanks to the many people who have assisted me in the preparation of this booklet, especially Mme Tamara Préaud and Mme Isabelle Laurin of the archives of the Manufacture Nationale de Sèvres, to Mrs Joan Wilson, archivist to the Duke of Wellington, for her help at Stratfield Saye, to Mrs Fiona Hirst for her painstaking work on the marks and the sources, to Miss Sue Service, Miss Pam Smith and Mr Rupert Harris in the V&A's Conservation Department; to Mr Hugh Sainsbury, Miss Christine Smith and Mr Charles Nichols for their excellent photography, and, of course, to the other members of the Department of Ceramics at the Victoria and Albert Museum.

Charles Truman
Department of Ceramics

Typeset by Hugh Wilson Typesetting, Norwich
Printed in England for Her Majesty's Stationery Office
by Penshurst Press Ltd, Tunbridge Wells, Kent
Designed by HMSO Graphic Design

ISBN 0 905209 24 9
7/82 Dd no 8219727

FOREWORD

The Sèvres *Service Egyptien* is without doubt the grandest example of French porcelain to have survived from the Empire period. Its massive architectural centrepiece and elegant accompaniments draw the same compliments today as they did during the manufacture of the service, when it was said to be both rich and beautiful as well as being simple and interesting. The fascinating history of the service, with its connections with Napoleon, Josephine and the first Duke of Wellington – to whom it was given by a grateful French monarch in 1818 – make it a splendid acquisition for the Nation for display at Apsley House. However, the problem of providing an appropriate setting was a knotty one. In the event the purchase of the Egyptian Service has acted as the trigger for a complete redecoration and casing of the Plate and China Room. The Department of the Environment has risen to the occasion with a magnificent new showcase, veneered in rosewood and carefully detailed to match the Iron Duke's own cases.

Roy Strong
Director

THE SÈVRES EGYPTIAN SERVICE

Fig. 1. Dominique Vivant, baron Denon, by P. Prudhon (Musée du Louvre)

The Sèvres *'Service Egyptien'* displayed at Apsley House, London, represents a collaboration of some of the most interesting and colourful figures in politics, the arts and the sciences of the early nineteenth century. The principals in the story of its production are the Emperor Napoleon himself, his wife Josephine, Alexandre Brongniart, one of the great figures in ceramic history, and the diplomat, courtier and artist Dominique Vivant, baron Denon; but they are supported by the architects Jean-Baptiste Le Peyre and Théodore Brongniart, by the painters Jacques-François-Joseph Swebach-Desfontaines, as well as the host of painters, gilders, modellers, repairers and turners at the Manufacture Impériale de Sèvres.

Vivant Denon, or de Non, as he signed his name until the Revolution, came to prominence at the court of Louis XV, where his wit and charm endeared him to the King, who appointed him *gentilhomme ordinaire du Roi* in 1769.[1] In the same year a play by Denon, *Julie, ou le bon père* was produced by

1. Judith Nowinski: *Baron Dominique Vivant Denon* (1970) p. 29.

5

the Comédie Française. In 1771 or '72[2] Vivant Denon embarked on a diplomatic career, being sent to the court of Catherine the Great at St Petersburg as *gentilhomme d'ambassade*. It was at this embassy that Denon is said to have met the *philosophe* Diderot. His stay in the Russian capital does not appear to have been an unqualified diplomatic success for he was expelled from the country in 1774.[3] In the following year Denon visited Switzerland whither he departed 'en artiste voyageur, uni de l'attirail complet du dessinateur et le portefeuille sous le bras, comme un peintre en quête de sites pittoresques'.[4] On his return to France he visited Ferney to see Voltaire with whom he seems to have developed a deep friendship.[5] He recorded his visit with a delightful engraving, 'Le dejeuné de Ferney' depicting Diderot's wife, his chambermaid 'la belle Agathe', the Jesuit M. Adam and Benjamin de Laborde gathered around the philosopher.[6]

In 1776 Denon joined the French embassy in Naplès where he remained for the following nine years. During this period he collaborated with the Abbé de St Non on his *Voyage pittoresque ou description des royaumes de Naples et de Sicile* (Paris, 1780 – 86) and with Henry Swinburne on *Travels in the Two Sicilies* (London, 1783 – 85) as well as preparing his own *Voyage en Sicile,* published in 1788. It was during this period that we first receive an indication of Denon's interest in ceramics and a connection with Sèvres. In 1785 he wrote to the comte d'Angivilliers that he possessed 'un collection de vases étrusques fort considerable, et peut-être la plus complète qui existe pour les formes'.[7] This collection of five hundred and twenty pieces was eventually acquired by d'Angivilliers for Sèvres.[8] In the same years Denon was expelled from the court at Naples, and returned to Paris, by way of Rome, but was in Venice by 1788, where he remained through the French Revolution in

2. Pierre Lelièvre, *Vivant Denon* (Paris, 1942) p. 18, n. 6, concludes that the date must have been 1771, but Nowinski, op.cit. p. 32 gives the following year.   3. Nowinski, op.cit. p. 36.

4. Albert de la Fizelière, *L'Oeuvre originale de Vivant Denon,* (Paris, 1862) p. 9, 'like a travelling artist, kitted out as a draftsman, with his portfolio under his arm, like a painter in search of picturesque views'.

5. La Fizelière, op.cit. pp. 9 – 17   6. Nowinski, op.cit. p. 41

7. Lalièvre, op.cit. p. 20

8. George Lechevallier-Chevignard, *La Manufacture de le Porcelaine de Sèvres,* (Paris, 1980) p. 98. I am grateful to Mrs Charlotte Gibbon for this reference.

1789, until the *serenissima* expelled all French residents in August 1792, when Denon moved first to Florence and then back to Paris.[9]

It was not a favourable time for a noble and suspected *emigré* to be in Paris. Denon sought protection from the painter Louis David whom he had known in Naples and who was an active supporter of the Revolution. Denon engraved David's 'Serment du Jeu de Paume' which, so to speak, proved that he was a good patriot.[10] The painter also obtained for his protegé the job of engraving the uniforms which were planned for civilian officers of the Republic.[11] Denon frequently attended the meetings of the revolutionary tribunal and sketched Danton, Fouquier-Tinville and Carrier, and on one occasion met Robespierre at the Committee for Public Safety. In 1793 Denon published *L'Oeuvre Priapique,* a group of engravings apparently inspired by the sexual practices of the ancient Pompeiians and depicting 'les attitudes pleines d'abandon de Mme Mosion' one of which is wittily signed 'Denon vidit 27 f 1787'.

There are several versions of how Denon and Bonaparte first met, but one, combining as it does at least two accounts, may be given here. At a ball given by Talleyrand the youthful Bonaparte had accepted a glass of lemonade from Denon, having been too shy to ask a servant for one himself. The two discussed the soldier's native Corsica at some length. As a friend of Josephine Beauharnais to whom he had been introduced by the miniaturist Jean-Baptiste Isabey, Denon was once again introduced to Bonaparte, now promoted General, but the latter disapproved of Denon's companion for the evening and failed to recognise his one-time benefactor until the conversation turned again to Corsica.[13]

9. Lalièvre, op.cit. p. 22

10. Roger Portalis & Henri Beraldi, *Les Graveurs du XVIIIᵉ Siècle,* (Paris, 1880 – 82) Vol. 1, 'Denon'.

11. La Fizelière, op.cit. section 16, 'Costumes Français.de la Convention'.

12. Nowinski, op.cit. p. 72 and n. 38

13. Nowinski, op.cit. p. 175 – 7.

In 1798 Bonaparte undertook his famous campaign in Egypt, an extravagant demonstration of power which in hindsight may be viewed as the most disastrous military manifestation of Egyptomania, that fascination with the mysteries of the Nile which has inspired Western minds since Roman times. Vivant Denon was anxious to join the group of scholars, architects and scientists which had gathered for the expedition but did not dare to approach the general himself. Josephine, fearing that her own entreaties on his behalf would be rejected, sought the assistance of Arnault, Bonaparte's secretary, to obtain a post for him. The general was delighted with the suggestion, admiring in Denon such an adventurous spirit for a man of fifty-one, and at once regretted that he had not engaged the services of a poet to record in epic verse the historic expedition that he was to undertake. Denon set sail from France on May 15, 1798, with General Defulga on board the frigate *La Junon*.[14] Throughout the ensuing campaign Vivant Denon astonished the soldiers that he accompanied with his irrepressible spirit and disregard for his own safety under fire. He described his journey and the campaign in the *Voyage dans la Basse et la Haute Egypte,* published by Didot *ainé* in two volumes (one quarto for the text and one large folio containing the plates) in 1802 with engravings of the large number of drawings with which Denon returned by Galien, Beltrand, Berthault, Pillement *fils,* and several others. In the introduction he complains of the problems created by the pursuit of an enemy mounted on horses. 'J'étois donc obligé quelquefois de passer rapidement sur les monuments les plus interessants; quelquefois de m'arrêter ou il m'y avoit rien à observer'. He continues that the 'dessins qui j'ai fait le plus souvent sur mon genou, ou debut, ou même à cheval: j'ai jamais pu en terminer un seul à ma volonté, puisque pendant toute une année je n'ai pas trouvé une seule table assez bien dressé pour y poser une règle'. Despite such difficulties, Denon's enthusiasm for Egyptian antiquities bursts from the pages, and it is clear that he conveyed his zeal to his companions for he writes, 'Si l'amour de l'antiquité a fait souvent de moi un soldat, la complaisance des soldats pour mes recherches en a fait souvent des antiquaires'.[15]

In the year that the *Voyage* was published Vivant Denon was appointed director of the Musée Napoleon, and, in 1803, of the Monnaie des Medailles. As such he oversaw all aspects of the arts. He advised painters such as David and Gerard on historical details, especially of the many battles at which he had been present and he even designed parades and state events as well as supervising more permanent structures such as the obelisk on the pont Neuf, the sculpture on the pont de la Concorde and pont d'Iena and the monument to his friend General Desaix in the place des Victoires.[16] It is not surprising therefore to find him acting as artistic adviser to the Manufacture Impériale at Sèvres where his name is first mentioned on January 25, 1805.

At the turn of the nineteenth century the factory at Sèvres had reached a particularly low ebb. Competition from the Paris factories and finally the Revolution had forced the former royal porcelain factory into a position of financial and artistic stagnation. In an attempt to revitalise the concern, Lucien Bonaparte, then Minister for the Interior, nominated Alexandre Brongniart as administrator on 15 May 1800, a post which he was to hold until his death in 1847. Still only thirty years old, Brongniart, who was by training a geologist and a former professor of natural history at the Ecole Centrale des Quatre Nations, at once set about a reorganisation of the factory and the disposal of old stock. He perfected a hard paste, still in use today, which fired with fewer casualties than the hard paste which had been in production at Sèvres since 1769, and he developed a new glaze. In the

14. Nowinski, op.cit. 79; La Fizelière, op.cit.. 37 – 8 and Lalièvre, op.cit. 23 – 4.
15. 'I was obliged therefore sometimes to speed past the most interesting monuments, at other times to stop where there was nothing for me to look at . . . drawings which were often made on my knee, or standing, or even from my horse: I never finished any as I would have wished, for during that whole year I never found a table flat enough to put a ruler on . . . If love of antiquities often made a solider of me, the soldiers' enjoyment of my researches often made antiquaries of them.'
16. Lalièvre, op.cit. p. 53.

1790s he had published a treatise on enamelling after studying the techniques in England, and several colours, particularly the 'beau bleu' which forms such a striking part of the *Service Egyptien,* and chrome green are attributed to him. Furthermore his travels as a geologist enabled him to collect a wide variety of pottery and porcelain that today forms the basis of the Musée de Céramique at Sèvres, a catalogue of which he published shortly before his death.[17]

Still with the Egyptian campaign, and no doubt the success of his *Voyage* still in mind, Vivant Denon wrote to Alexandre Brongniart at Sèvres on 26 Pluviose year XIII, 'Il m'est venu dans le tête un charmant grouppe [sic] égyptien d'une facile exécution, pour porter des fruits crus, glacés ou secs et qui tout à la fois entrerait dans le service et le decoration du surtout. Dites-moi si vous pouvez avec quelque pureté faire de l'architecture: dites-moi si dans les fûts de colonnes vous pouriez conserver les lignes bien filées . . . avec un succés assuré dans cette partie, nous obtiendrons un surtout tout à fait monumental'.[18] Thus, the idea of a service and centrepiece based on the

17. Pierre Verlet, Serge Grandjean and Marcelle Brunet, *Sèvres,* 2 vols, (Paris, 1953) pp. 54 – 55 and 63.
18. Archives of the Manufacture Nationale de Sèvres (afterwards referred to as AMNS). T1.L6.D2. 'The idea has come to me for a charming Egyptian group, easy to make, to carry fresh, glacé or dried fruit and which at the same time would be part of the service and of the centrepiece. Tell me if you could make architecture with some accuracy: tell me if you could maintain the strict lines of columns . . . If you can assure success with that, we will get a really monumental centrepiece.'

Pl. 1. One of a pair of *sucriers,* designed by Jean-Charles-Nicholas Brachard, and gilt by Micaud (C.127 & A–1979)

Pl. 2. One of the pair of *confituriers,* gilt by Micaud
        (C.131–1979)

Pl. 3.

a. *Assiette à monter,* painted by Deparais, on a ground
   by Godin and gilt by Boullemier le jeune (C.125f–
   1979)

b. *Ruines d'Hieraconpolis,* painted by J.-F.-J. Swebach
   and possibly gilt by Micaud (C.124/8–1979)

c. *La Fête dans le Harem,* painted by J.-F.-J. Swebach,
   gilt by Micaud, 1811 (C.124/37–1979)

d. *Vue d'une Mosquée près Rosette,* painted by J.-F.-J.
   Swebach, and gilt by Micaud, 1811 (C.124/21-1979)

a.

b.

c.

d.

Fig. 3. The Temple of Dendera; engraving by Baltard after a drawing by Denon (Pl. 39)

Vue géométrale du Portique du Temple de Tentyris.

engravings after the drawings of Vivant Denon was born. In Prairial (June) of that year, Denon suggested that the architect Jean-Baptiste Le Peyre, or Lepère, should be consulted for designs for the surtout.[19] Lepère had also accompanied Napoleon to Egypt, where his prime concern, apart from several grand buildings in Cairo, was with charting the ancient canal across the isthmus of Suez. In his youth Lepère had been to Constantinople to build a canon foundry and his metallurgical experience won him the task, with Gondouin, of constructing the bronze column in the place Vendôme in celebration of Napoleon's German campaigns. However, in 1802 his reputation had been made with the building of Malmaison. On 27 Brumaire year XIV (17 November 1805) Brongniart was able to write to Denon that 'Monsieur Le Peyre nous a donné un dessin très net et très soigné des temples du surtout'.[20] The design, which no longer survives, was based on the temples of Philae, Dendera and Edfu, the pylon and the sacred rams of the temple of Karnak at Thebes, the colossal figures of Memnon, and the obelisks at Luxor.

19. P. Arizzoli-Clémentel, 'Les surtouts imperiaux en porcelaine de Sèvres, 1804 – 14', *Keramik-Freunde der Schweiz, Mitteilungsblat,* Nr. 88, May 1976, p. 17.
20. AMNS. T2.L2.D5.

Fig. 4. The entry to Luxor; engraving by Baltard after a drawing by Denon (Pl. 50)

Plaster models were made from this design by the sculptors Brachard *le jeune,* Liance *ainé* and Oger, under the supervision of Brachard *ainé*,[21] and moulds were made by Paulin and Legendre.[22] The models are still to be found at Sèvres today. The records of 'Travaux Extraordinaire' show, for example, that Paulin was paid 5 francs for the moulds of the *sucrier* with an additional 4 francs for the egyptian head which forms the handle. It is clear that the manufacture and firing of the temples which made up the surtout presented a difficult task, the model of Philae alone took four months, and indeed one that might have proved impossible without Brongniart's improved hard-paste porcelain. The administrator of the factory constantly sought guidance from Denon who wrote, on 26 April 1807, commiserating over the problems of constructing the central model of the temple of Philae, adding 'mais j'en reviens encore à cela qu'il suffit qu'une chose soit faisable pour qu'elle ait été faite à la Manufacture Impériale. Si vous ne faisez rien de ce genre, d'autres feraient tout ce que vous faites et ce ne serait plus la

21. AMNS. Va'17   22. AMNS. Va'15.

23. AMNS. T3.L1.D3. 'But I come back again to the fact that if it is possible for something to be made, then the Imperial Factory can make it. If you make nothing of this kind, then others will make what

Fig. 5. *La Fère dans la Harem*, engraving by Garreau after a drawing by Denon (Pl. 112)

première Manufacture de l'Europe. Courage donc, car j'ai promis à l'Empereur qu'il trouverait le service fait à son retour' (from Germany).[23] In the same letter, Denon interestingly expresses a preference for soft paste porcelain, no longer made at Sèvres. The centrepiece which resulted from the efforts of Brongniart, his modellers and repairers, is one of the greatest ever produced in porcelain. Stretching for over twenty-two feet in length it comprises seventeen separate units of biscuit porcelain mounted on tôle peinte in imitation of 'granite rose égyptien'.[24] At the centre stands the temple of Philae flanked by four obelisks. Two smaller temples, comprising elements from Dendera and Edfu, complete the central group. These are joined by colonnades to two pylons, or *môles*, those monumental Egyptian gateways, in this instance modelled on those at Karnak. The outer groups are composed of four seated figures, the so-called figures of Memnon, paired at each end, at the head of avenues of sacred rams set on rectangular plinths. The temples, pylons, obelisks and colonnades are decorated with a plethora of hieroglyphs, which although in imitation of the Egyptian are unreadable, having been grouped together at random, before such things

you make and you will no longer be Europe's premier factory. Courage then, because I have promised the Emperor that the service will be completed on his return.

24. AMNS. T4.L2.D4.

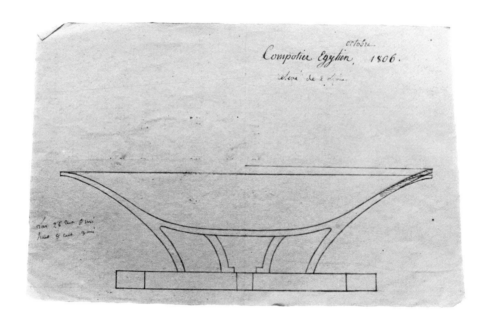

Compotier Egyptien, 1806.

were adequately understood.[25] The biscuit was attached to the tôle by M. Quinton, a locksmith from St Cloud, and the whole was to be mounted on a plateau 'd'aprés l'avis de Monsieur Denon, il devrait être en tôle peinte et vernié imitant le granit gris, il serait tout uni sans bronze ni dorure,[25] although originally a gilt-bronze plateau by Thomire had been suggested. The plateau was ordered from the Manufacture de Vernis sur Metaux et Laque Français (Messrs Montcloux, Janvry and Flamart) of 10, rue Martel, Paris. Brongniart announced that 'le surtout égyptien est enfin terminé' on 25 July 1808, although the plateau had not been delivered, and was not completed until some years later.

The dessert service which accompanied the centrepiece was no less magnificent. According to a list at Sèvres it comprised seventy-two plates, twelve *compotiers,* four *sucriers,* two *confituriers,* four *seaux à glace,* four *corbeilles,*

25. Arizzoli-Clémentel, op.cit. p. 22. 'following the advice of M. Denon, it was to be of metal painted and varnished like grey granite all over with neither bronze nor gilding'.
26. AMNS. T4.L2.D4.
27. AMNS. Vy fols 61 verso and 62.

18

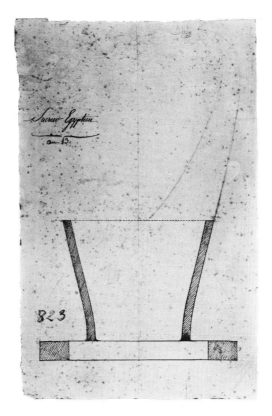

and four Egyptian figures carrying dishes.[27] The plates were described at
the factory as 'fond beau bleu, hieroglyphes en or Dessus le fond, Sujets de la
Compagne d'Egypte, peint à la Sepia pas Mr Swebach, d'apres l'ouvrage de
Mr Denon'. The painter referred to was Jacques-François-Joseph Swebach-
Desfontaines who was granted the unusual privilege of being allowed to
sign his work with the single word 'Swebach', or simply 'Sw', scratched
through the enamel. Each plate bears a different scene of Egypt after an
engraving in Denon's *Voyage dans la Basse et la Haute Egypte.* The borders,
again after Denon, were designed by Théodore Brongniart, father of the
Sèvres administrator, who was paid 2,400 francs for designs in 1806, and
gilt by Micaud *fils,* Boullemier, Constant, Godin *le jeune* and Coitel.
Brongniart *père* was a distinguished architect who, having fallen in and out
of favour with a rapidity not unusual during the Revolutionary years, was

Fig. 8. *Seau à glace du Service Egyptien,* design in the archives of the Manufacture Nationale de Sèvres

appointed *inspecteur-general des bâtiments* in 1801. His most notable memorial is the Paris Bourse which he designed in 1808 but never saw completed. Each plate was valued at 200 francs. The *compotiers,* a design for which dated 1806 is preserved in the factory (fig. 6), were painted with signs of the zodiac by Deparais.[28] The *sucriers* were designed by Jean-Charles-Nicholas Brachard (fig. 7), after illustrations by Denon, and were valued at 280 francs each with the gilding alone costing over half this amount. A design for a *seau à glace égyptien* at Sèvres (fig. 8) is signed 'Alex B', probably for Alexandre Brachard who also modelled the Egyptian figures. With typical business sense Brongniart wrote to Vivant Denon, 'Mr. Dumont et d'autres sculpteurs me demandent, pour faire la figure égyptienne qui porte une vasque, un prix qui me semble trop elevé; je me suis decidé à la faire faire à Sèvres par M. Brachard, notre sculpteur. Comme il a pris quelques conseils

28. Arizzoli-Clémentel, op.cit. n.212.

Fig. 9. *Corbeille à Palme,* hard paste porcelain, painted in enamels, silvered and gilt; assembled by Benoit Chanou, painted by Godin and gilt by Constant (C.130–1979)

de Monsieur Chaudet, et qu'il y a mis beaucoup de soin, j'ai lieu d'espéré que vous serez satisfait.'[29] The figures were modelled from No. 32 in plate 135 in Denon's *Voyage,* entitled 'Peintures dans les tombeaux des Rois à Thèbes'.[30] The designs of the *confituriers* and the two sorts of *corbeilles* were also taken from Denon, plates 115, no. 1 and 59, nos. 7 and 8 respectively.

The completed service was destined as a present to Tsar Alexander I of Russia. The Grand Maréchal du Palais, Duroc, wrote to Sèvres in September 1807 enquiring 'où est le service égyptien: s'il était prêt, S.M. l'enverrait aussi' (with the *service Olympique*).[31] Having been promised at Tilsit in 1807, the service was eventually delivered in October 1808 at Erfurt although it was not unpacked there but sent on to St Petersburg.[32] Brongniart, worried by the speed at which the service had been packed,

29. AMNS. T2.L2.D5. 'For the Egyptian figure carrying a dish, Mr Dumont and the other sculptors asked a price that seemed to me to be too high; I decided to have the thing done by M. Brachard, our sculptor. As he has sought the advice of M. Chaudet, and taken much care, I have every reason to hope that you will be satisfied'.

30. Joan Wilson, 'Little Gifts Keep Friendship Alive', *Apollo,* July 1975, p. 51, fig. 2.

31. Arizzoli-Clémentel, p. 17.

32. Arizzoli-Clémentel, op.cit. p. 19 – 20.

wrote 'Si quelques pièces de ce surtout se derangeaient en route, on pourrait les recoller et les rajuste avec du plàtre fin et gommé auquel on donne la teinte de la porcelaine en y ajoutant un peu de bleu de prusse . . . quand il sera sale, on lui redonnera la première blancheur en le lavant avec une brosse, de l'eau et du sablon trés fin, il ne faut point employer de savon'.[33] The service, which differs slightly from the list given by the factory in that it includes the *assiettes à monter* decorated with scarabs and only two *seaux à glace*,[34] is in the care of the state Ceramic Museum, at Kuskuvo near Moscow.

While the service was being prepared at Sèvres the Empress Josephine had visited the factory to see its progress. She had been, according to Brongniart, 'extrèmement contente',[35] and her approval of the design is indicated by the fact that when, as a present following their divorce on 16 December 1809, Napoleon offered her a gift of 30,000 francs of Sèvres porcelain, she took little time in ordering a similar service. On 1st January 1810 Brongniart was invited to Malmaison to discuss the gift by Josephine's *Secretaire des commandements,* Deschamps.

The order appears at the factory on 15 February 1810, listed as

'Service dit Egyptien fond beau bleu, Vues d'Egypte &c.
  72 Assiettes
  12 d° pour assiettes à monter
  12 Compotiers
   2 Sucriers
   2 Confituriers
   2 Seaux a Glaces
   4 Corbeilles
   4 figures Egyptiennes avec vasques
  Le Surtout complet'

with a total value of 34,780 francs. The following day the order is noted under the heading of Government presents, although in a slightly different

33. AMNS. P6 1 L1, Arizzoli-Clémental, op.cit. p. 21. 'If some pieces of the centrepiece become displaced in transit you can readjust them and stick them back with a mixture of fine plaster and glue with a little Prussian Blue added to give it the colour of porcelain . . . When it gets dirty, the original whiteness can be regained by washing it with a brush, some water and very fine scouring sand, never use soap'.
34. Joan Wilson, op.cit. p. 53.

form, there being only two *figures avec vasques,* and together with 36 plates painted with different landscapes, a *Cabaret Egyptien* and a *Cabaret des Femmes Célebres.* It here made clear that Josephine would pay the difference between the 30,000 francs allowed her and the total cost of 56,134 francs of the whole order.[36]

It is possible that Brongniart anticipated the order following his meeting in January with Deschamps, for in the same month the *tourneur* Descoins was paid for work on '8 vasques pour les figures Egyptiens' and Lemoine, a *garnisseur,* or Mathias Chanou, whose name is written beneath, provided '1 corbeille lautus du S(ervice) E(gyptien) for which he was paid 110 francs.[37] In fact, the second Egyptian Service does not contain a 'corbeille lautus', whose form is derived from Denon, pl. 59, no. 8, a pair of which appear with the Russian example. The two baskets which accompany the second service are of a form known as *'Corbeille à palme'* (fig. 9) and derive from Denon pl. 59, no. 7. Although Legendre was given the task of looking out the moulds and models in February 1810, work did not begin in earnest until May or June.[38] The records at Sèvres give details of the various jobs undertaken by the craftsmen in the different shops of the factory. For example, the repairer Godin *père* began work in May on the side of one of the pylon gateways of the centrepiece for which he was paid 60 francs, and he continued working on the various parts of the centrepiece until 30 June 1812.[39] He was engaged on columns and cornices for the three temples, for the colonnades, for the walls and bases of the temples, on the obelisks and on the sphinxes (actually rams). Other repairers included Bougon *ainé* who worked on the *sucriers,* the *confituriers,* as well as on the centrepiece, from March 1810, Augustin Liance (columns, pylons, and, in April 1812, one of the figures), Thévenot (plinths, columns and capitals), Mathias Chanou (cornices, pylons and baskets), and Benoit Chanou (cornices and baskets). The turners were d'Avignon *père* (*sucriers* and *confituriers*), Thion *père*

35. AMNS. T3.L1.D5, letter dated 10 April 1807.
36. AMNS. V r.r.' I fol. 120.
37. AMNS. VA 18 fols. 53 and 123.
38. Arizzoli-Clémentel, p. 27.
39. AMNS, VA 18 fol 93, and VA 19 fol.94 ff.

(supports for the Egyptian figures, and a large number of plates), Louis Davignon (*compotiers*), Pétion (plaques for the temples) and two apprentices Mascret and Frédéric Marchand who seem to have worked mainly on the columns.[40]

Firing the pieces of the centrepiece began in April 1810 with one of the pylons and appears to have continued at least until 28 May 1812, although one 'môle du Temple Egyptien' was fired as late as 2nd September 1812.[41] Several specific firings are noted in the Journal des fourniers,[42] but the carefully kept kiln records show how many pieces were fired, how many were satisfactory and how many were rejected. For example, the records for 8 May 1810 show that four *sucriers E(gyptiens)* were fired, two passing as good and two rejected.[43] In the main, however, the firings do not appear to have presented too many problems at this second attempt to make architecture in porcelain.

Painting and gilding the rest of the service began in May 1810 when Micaud *fils* was paid 140 francs for the hieroglyphs on four plates, but the records for the painting and gilding shop show no further work until January 1811.[44] Throughout 1811, and up until April 1812, Micaud is employed in gilding Théodore Brongniart's borders to the plates. In July and August 1811 he was paid for gilding the *compotiers* which he painted the following November (figs. 82 – 93). In August 1811 he was paid 33 francs each for 'le decore' of the two *seaux à glace,* and a further 100 francs each 'pour le peinture du Bas Reliefs hieroglyphique et Sujets' on the same pieces in December of that year.[45] In between times Mme Asselin is recorded as having given the gilding a first polish in September. In January 1812 Micaud gave both the *seaux* their final burnishing and touching up. Micaud was also responsible for gilding the *sucriers* for which he was paid 100 francs

40. AMNS, VA 18 and VA 19.
41. AMNS. VC' 6 fol. 104 to VC' 7 fol. 44 and VC' 7 fol. 53.
42. AMNS. Vuu' 1, 1806 – 14, fols. 121 – 136.
43. AMNS. Vj.
44. AMNS. Vj 17 fol. 34.
45. AMNS. Vj 18 fols. 34 ff.

each in October 1811, with an additional 3 francs each for work on the heads in January 1812. In October 1811 he gilt the two *confituriers,* at 16 francs each, which he completed by burnishing the covers for a second time in January 1812. His last work on the service appears to have been gilding the bowls carried by the Egyptian figures in April 1812.[46]

The *assiettes à monter* (pl.3 & fig. 94) appear from the records to have been gilt before painting, as the *seaux à glace* and the *compotiers.* In October 1811 Boullemier *le jeune* gilt four of them and Constant the remaining eight, while in January 1812 the *metteur en fond* Godin applied 'le fond café' and Deparais painted the scarabs.[47] The *corbeilles* present a more complicated case since there were an additional four pieces made for Josephine and supplied separately in 1812.[48] The ground colour 'Brun et la granite' was applied to a pair by Godin in November 1811, although they were not completed until the new year when 'granite' had changed to 'fond marbre'. The same craftsmen painted four socles for baskets in March 1812. The gilder M. Constant decorated three baskets in February 1812, one with 'fond chrome' which may account for the unusual finish to the lower section of the baskets in the second service.[49] Those in Russia are brightly burnished gold.

The largest group in the service comprises the sixty-six plates painted with views of Egypt after the engraving of drawings made by Denon in 1798. As with the first service, the scenes were painted by Jacques-François-Joseph Swebach-Desfontaines, whose signature appears on many of the pieces (full details of all the marks and signatures are given in Appendix 1). Swebach began painting in January 1811 and continued on and off until April or May 1812, sometimes painting as many as twelve plates per month. The documents list seventy-six plates of which sixty-seven survive: one is

46. AMNS. Vj 19.
47. AMNS. Vj 18 and 19.
48. Arizzoli-Clémentel, n. 306.
49. AMNS. Vj 19. Scientific examination of the ground revealed a quantity of silver, now oxidised grey, but no trace of chromium.

still at Sèvres in the Musée National de Céramique. So far as it has been possible to match the plates with the descriptions in the records at Sèvres, the illustrations in black and white of the plates have been set out in the order in which they were painted. However there are one or two anomalies and difficulties. A plate entitled 'Ruines d'Hieraconpolis' was said to have been painted in May 1811 but bears the date 1812 and four plates painted in February 1812 are all said to be of the 'Temple de Tentyris' (Dendera), without any further identification to show which was painted first. Swebach was paid the sum of 50 francs per plate.[50] The gilding of the plates was largely carried out by Micaud, but Constant and Boullemier *le jeune* are both recorded as having gilt hieroglyphs on plates during 1811 and 1812. The *'garniture'* and retouching of the gilding was done by Vandé *aîné* and the title of each plate was written on the reverse by the gilder Legrand,[51] except for one plate in March 1812 by Deparais.

It is clear that Josephine followed the production of the *Service Egyptien* with interest and impatience. As early as 18 March 1810 Brongniart received a letter from the *Intendant* Daru enquiring where the service which the Empress had ordered was. Further enquiries followed in November 1810 and June 1811,[52] and Brongniart replied in encouraging terms giving wildly optimistic accounts of the progress on the service.

The service was eventually delivered to Malmaison on 1 April 1812 carried in six litters by twelve men.[53] It is clear that the tôle peinte plateau did not accompany the service. M. Tavernier, who had succeeded Messrs Montcloux, Janvry and Flamart at 10, rue Martel wrote on 8 February apologising to Brongniart that the plateau would not be ready in time. Indeed it does not appear at Sèvres until April 1818 when a 'plateau en tolle vernis et peint au granis, composé de cinq parties, destiné pour le surtout

50. AMNS. Vj 18 and 19.   51. AMNS. Vj 19, fol. 169.
52. Arizzoli-Clémentel, p. 24 – 25.   53. Joan Wilson, op.cit. p. 59.

du Service Egyptien' is mentioned in a 'feuille d'appreciation' of pieces which had arrived in the saleroom.

However as Brongniart wrote later, the service did not please the Empress: 'quelques jours après S.M. m'a fait l'honneur de me demander et m'a dit qu'après un plus mûr examen, Elle trouvoit le service top sévère et qu'Elle désiroit en avoir autre dont Elle me donnerait les dessins'.[54] This is supported by another letter from Brongniart to Baron Devaux dated 8 July 1814, where he goes on to say that a more elegant design for a new service was to be supplied by Louis-Martin Berthault,[55] a protégé of Josephine's who designed the gardens of Malmaison, and who enjoyed considerable popularity at this period. The Egyptian Service was returned to Sèvres. In the same letter Brongniart complained at the way events had affected the factory. Josephine had spent over 3000 francs of the money allowed her, leaving only a credit of 26,606 francs. He continued, 'Le service égyptien qui existe encore dans nôtre magasin est de 35,020 francs sans compter le plateau en tôle vernissée qui a été commander à Monsieur Tavernier pas order de S.M. qui a été fait et qui est encore entre les mains de ce fabricant . . . Enfin, les credits ouverts sous le gouvernement de l'empereur Napoléon out été annulès. Je me pourrois donc pas me permettre de livrer sans de nouveaux ordres les porcelaines nécessaires pour parfaire la valeur du présent de 30,000 Frs ordonne par l'empereur Napoleon'.[56] No mention is found again in the records at Sèvres of the *Service Egyptien*, save for a letter from M. Tavernier dated 3 February 1817 concerning the plateau,[56] until 20 March 1818.

After Waterloo, the first Duke of Wellington was installed in Paris as the commander of the army occupying France. At a dinner given by the Duke in March 1818 it is evident that he and the French King Louis XVIII had

54. Arizzoli-Clémentel, op.cit. p. 25.

55. A copy of this letter, the property of M. Théophile Briant, was kindly shown to me by Mme Préaud in the archives of the Manufacture Nationale de Sèvres.

56. The Egyptian Service which is still in our shop is valued at 35,020 francs, not including the plateau of toleware which was ordered from M. Tavernier on her majesty's instructions, completed and is still in the hands of the manufacturer. Finally the credits opened by Napoleon's government were cancelled. I could not therefore permit myself to release the porcelain comprised in the Emperor's commission of 30,000 francs without new orders. Arizzoli-Clémentel, n. 286.

discussed the relative merits of the old (soft paste) and the new (hard paste) porcelain. Since he wished to keep on friendly terms with the man who had assured his restoration to the throne, the King wrote on 20 March 1818 to offer him 'quelques assiettes' and closed with the sentiment in rather broken English 'Do little gifts – keep friendship alive'.[57]

An instruction dated the same day was sent from the comte de Pradel, *directeur général du ministère de la Maison du Roy,* to Alexandre Brongniart at Sèvres, informing him that the King wished the *Service Egyptien* to be sent without delay to the Tuileries. Pradel expressed a fear that the service would be considered unfashionable but such a consideration does not appear to have worried the King. It was, in any case, not the first time that the Egyptian Service had been suggested as a royal gift. In September 1817 it had been considered as a present to Cardinal Consalvi, secretary of state of Pius VII.[58] Brongniart complied with the order immediately and we find at Sèvres the record of delivery to 'Sa Grace M. le Duc de Wellington' dated 21 March 1818:

Service Egyptien, fond beau bleu, frise d'hieroglyphes en or. Vues d'Egypte peint en brun au milieu des assiettes.

Savoir	Peinture et dorure		Sculpture
66 assiettes avec vues	200	13,200	
12 assiettes à monter	60	720	
12 compotiers	120	1,440	
2 sucriers	280	560	
2 glacieres	450	900	
4 figures avec vasques	250	200	800
2 corbeilles	350	700	
2 confituriers	140	280	

Surtout:
Au milieu le temple de Philae; sur les deux côtes, deux temples, celui de Tentyris et Etfou; deux môles; quatre parties de colonnades liant les temples avec les môles, quatre autre parties de sphynx avec figures de Memnon terminant de surtout; quatre obélisques.

16,000

57. This letter which is preserved at Stratfield Saye is reproduced in full by Joan Wilson, op.cit. p. 60

1 grand plateau en tôle peint en granit pour supporter le surtout

1,500

Le 20 Aout 1819 addressé un facture à Monsieur le Comte de Pradel en sollicitant le paiement

Total pieces peinte   18,000

Total sculpture   18,300

Total   36,300

Included with the service were seventeen cardboard and green waxed paper covers. To judge from the construction of these, they were intended to protect the centrepeice when it was set out but not in use. They bear the mark MFB in monogram enclosed in a triangle surrounded by the legend 'Brévet d'invention à Strasbourg'.

Thus the *Service Egyptien* joined the other services which admiring monarchs showered on the first Duke of Wellington. However Brongniart had to wait for a further two years before he was finally paid,[60] ten years after the commission was originally placed with Sèvres, and fifteen years after the design had been conceived.

The service remained in the possession of the Dukes of Wellington until June 1979 when an opportunity arose for the Victoria and Albert Museum to acquire it for the nation and for the service to take its place alongside other tributes paid to the victor of Waterloo at his London residence, Apsley House.

Charles Truman
1982

58. Arizzoli-Clémentél, p. 27 and note 288.   59. AMNS. V bb5 fol. 15 vo.
60. Arizzoli-Clémentel, loc.cit.

ADDITIONAL REFERENCES

Marcel Gastineau, 'Denon et la Manufacture de Sèvres', *La Revue de l'Art,* LXIII, 1933, pp. 21 – 42.

Serge Grandjean, 'L'Influence Egyptienne a Sèvres' *Genootschap voor Napoleontische Studien,* September, 1955, pp. 99 – 105.

Serge Grandjean, 'The Wellington-Napoleon relics' *Connoisseur,* May 1959, pp. 223 – 230.

Philipe Julien, 'Napoleon sous l'empire des pharoans' *Connaissance des Arts,* 118, December, 1961, pp. 124 –132.

Sèvres, Museé National de Céramique, *Les Grands Service de Sèvres,* 25 May – 29 July 1951, No. 22.

London, Arts Council of Great Britain. *The Age of Neo-Classicism,* Victoria & Albert Museum, 1972, No. 1420.

Charles Truman, 'Emperor, King and Duke' *Connoisseur,* November, 1979, pp. 148 – 155.

Fig. 11. Detail of the centrepiece, showing the pylon, figures and sacred rams modelled on those at Karnak (C.132–1979)

THE CENTREPIECE

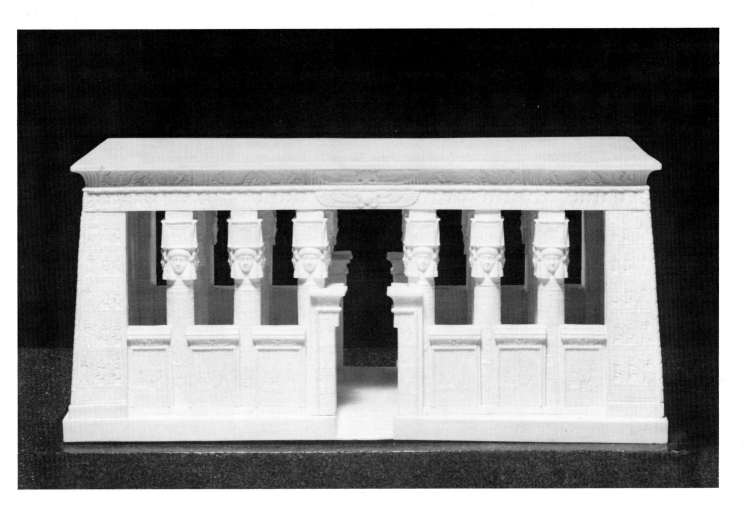

Fig. 12. The Temple of Philae from the centrepiece
        (C.132–1979)
Fig. 13. Temple of Dendera from the centrepiece
        (C.132–1979)

Fig. 14. Seated figure from the centrepiece (C.132–1979)

34

Fig. 15. Sacred ram
from the avenues of the
centrepiece (C.132–1979)

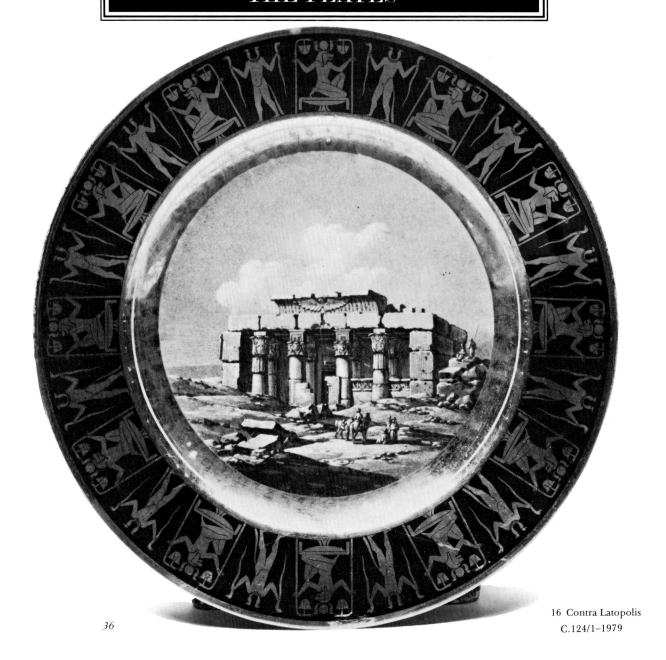

16 Contra Latopolis
C.124/1–1979

17. Vue d'un Temple de Thèbes à Kournou   C.124/2–1979

18. Habitation Nubienne près les Cataractes   C.124/3–1979

19. Ruines d'un Temple à Syéné   C.124/4–1979

20. Assemblée de Cheykhs   C.124/5–1979

21. Temple de Latopolis ou Esné   C.124/6–1979

22. Marchands de Macaroni   C.124/7–1979

23. Ruines d'Hieraconopolis   C.124/8–1979

24. Cataracte Du Nil   C.124/9–1979

25. Le Typhonium d'Apollinopolis   C.124/10–1979

26. Karavanseray   C.124/11–1979

27. Vue de Djirdich   C.124/12–1979

28. Entrée de Louqssor   C.124/13–1979

29. Vue de Qarnâq   C.124/14–1979

30. Le Vieux Caire   C.124/15–1979

31. Le Sphynx près les Pyramides   C.124/16–1979

32. Temple voisin d'Esné ou Latopolis   C.124/17–1979

33. Dyëbéléin ou les deux montagnes   C.124/18–1979

34. Tente d'Arabes C.124/19–1979

35. Vue d'Eléphatine   C.124/20–1979

36. Vue d'une Mosquée près Rossette   C.124/21–1979

37. Ruines d'oxyrynchus à Bénécé   C.124/22–1979

38. Déïr beyâdh le Couvent Blanc   C.124/23–1979

39. Vue de Philoé   C.124/24–1979

40. Karavanseray   C.124/25–1979

41. Ruines d'un Temple près Chnubis   C.124/26–1979

42. Bivouac   C.124/27–1979

43. Tombeaux Musulmans en brique   C.124/28–1979

44. Vue des ruines d'Ombos   C.124/29–1979

45. Vue de Zaoùyéh   C.124/30–1979

46. Vue des ruines de Chnubis   C.124/31–1979

47. Vue pittoresque du village de Qouss et du monument que l'on voit au milieu de la place
C.124/32–1979

48. Embrasement de Salmie   C.124/33–1979

49. Vue de Boulac   C.124/34–1979

50. Statues dites de Memnon   C.124/35–1979

51. Cimetière des Mamlouks à l'Est du Caire
          C.124/36–1979

52. La Fête dans le Harem   C.124/37–1979

53. Autre Vue d'un Temple d'Hermontis   C.124/38–1979

54. Le Memnonium   C.124/39–1979

55. Vue de l'isle de Philoé de l'est à l'ouest   C.124/40–1979

56. Vue de l'intérieur de la Mosquée de St. Athanase   C.124/41–1979

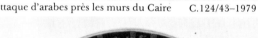

57. Vue de l'Isle de Philoé   C.124/42–1979

58. Attaque d'arabes près les murs du Caire   C.124/43–1979

59. Temple de Hermontis   C.124/44–1979

60. Palais et Temples de Thêbes à Medynet-à-bou
C.124/45–1979

61. Fours Egyptiens   C.124/46–1979

62. Vue de Zaòuyèh   C.124/47–1979

63. Arbre auquel on fait des offrandes   C.124/48–1979

64. Jardin de l'institute du Caire   C.124/49–1979

65. Tombeau Egyptien à Lycopolis   C.124/50–1979

66. Ruines du Temple d'Hermopolis   C.124/51–1979

67. Le Memnonium à Thêbes   C.124/52–1979

68. Pyramide d'Ellaboun   C.124/53–1979

69. Pyramide de Méidoûin   C.124/54–1979

70. Vue de Siut ou Osiot   C.124/55–1979

71. Sépultures arabes à Zaoye   C.124/56–1979

72. Vue de Bennissuéf   C.124/57–1979

73. Ruines d'un des Temples de l'isle d'Eléphantine
                          C.124/58–1979

74. La dernière Pyramide en Remontant le Nil   C.124/59–1979

75. Temple de Tentyris   C.124/60–1979

76. Temple de Tentyris   C.124/61–1979

77. Temple de Tentyris   C.124/62–1979

78. Temple de Tentyris   C.124/63–1979

79. Ruines de la Porte d'un Temple d'Eléphantine
C.124/64–1979

80. Carriere de Granite   C.124/65–1979

81. Ruines des Temples d'Eléphantine C.124/66–1979

Fig. 82. – Fig. 93. Twelve *Compotiers,* made by Louis
Davignon, painted with the signs of the Zodiac
and gilt by Micaud (C.126-k–1979)

Fig. 94. *Assiette à monter*, painted by Deparais on a ground by Godin and gilt by Constant (C.125–1979)

The sources of design and the marks

PLATES Title	after Denon pl.	border pl.	MARKS: incised	in green	in gold	in red (on most items the legend 'M.Imple' has been erased)
Contra Latopolis	53.2		10[1] ʃ[2]	24.j.v.	4 fv M fils 18m 15av	de Sevres 1811. V.D.
Vue d'un Temple de Thébes à Kournou	41.6	116.5	10 DC[3]	25.ot	M fils 4 fv. 16m 15av	de Sevres 1811. V.D.
Habitation Nubienne près les Cataractes	69.3	116.3	10 ʃ[4]	24.j.v.	4.D.bre. M fils 15av 15Jv.	de Sevres 1811. V.D.
Ruines d'un Temple à Syéné	66.1		9[5] DC	24	4 fv M fils 18m 15av	de Sevres 1811. V.D.
Assemblée de Cheykhs	78.1	116.10	8[6] ʃ	24.j.v.	4.D.bre. M fils	de Sevres 1811. V.D.
Temple de Latopolis ou Esné	53.1	131.1	67[7] ⅃ ⱷ[8]	24	16 1 M f 15av	de Sevres 1811. V.D.
Marchands de Macaroni	85.1	126.5	9 ʃ	24.j.v.	4fev M fils 15av 18m	de Sevres 1811. V.D.
Ruines d'Hieraconpolis	54 bis.2	114.37 & 113	OZ[9] DⱢ[10]	15.j.11	16 m	de Sevres 1812. V.D.
Cataracte du Nil	69.1	116.9	10 DC	25.ot	M.fils 4fv 15av 22 f	de Sevres 1811. V.D.
Le Typhonium d'Apollinpolis	57.1	116.8	10 DC	25.ot	M.fils 4fv 6m 4m	de Sevres 1811. V.D.
Kàravànserày	27.1	129.3	9 DC	28.j.v.	M.or 1 avril 15av	
Vue de Djirdich	34.2	116.4	10 CC[11]	25.ot	M.fils 4fv 6m 4m	de Sevres 1811. V.D.
Entrée de Louqssor	50.1	116.2	9 ʃ	24.7.v.	4 D.bre.M fils 6m 15Jv	de Sevres 1811. V.D.
Vue de Qarnâq	43.3	114.7	9 DC	24	4fev M fils 18m 6m	de Sevres 1811.
Le Vieux Caire	22.2	132.1	10 ʃ	24.j.v.	4 D bre M fils 15 fv	de Sevres 1811. V.D.
Le Sphynx près les Pyramides	26 bis.1	122.5	10 DC	24.j.v.	4 fv M fils 15 av 18 m	de Sevres 1811. V.D.

PLATES Title	after Denon pl.	border pl.	MARKS: incised	in green	in gold	in red (on most items the legend 'M.Imple' has been erased)
Temple voisin d'Esné ou Latopolis	52.1	132.2	10 ꝯ	24.j.v.	4 D bre M fils 15 av 15 Jv	de Sevres 1811. V.D.
Dyëbéléin ou les deux montagnes	52.2	116.1	9 DC	24.j.v.	4 D bre M fils 15 av 15 Jv	de Sevres 1811. V.D.
Tente d'Arabes	54.1	117.4	9 DC	24	M 4 fv 1 av	de Sevres 1811. V.D.
Vue d'Eléphantine	63,2	117.1	8 ℒ Ɗ	24	M 4 fv 1 av	de Sevres 1811. V.D.
Vue d'une Mosquée près Rossette	14.1	117.2	7 ꝯ	24	M 4 fv 1 av	de Sevres 1811. V.D.
Ruines d'Oxyrynchus à Bénécé	31.2	117.3	10 ꝯ	24	M 4 fv 1 av	de Sevres 1811. V.D.
Dëïr beyâdh le Couvent Blanc	32.2	117.6	10 ʃ	24	L.M. 4 fv 1 av	de Sevres 1811. V.D.
Vue de Philoé	63.3	117.5	8 ʃ C	24	M 4 fv 1 av	de Sevres 1811. V.D.
Karavanseray	34.1		10 ꝯ	24	4 fv M fils 6m 18m	de Sevres 1811. V.D.
Ruines d'un Temple près Chnubis	75.1	119.18 &19&20	7 ꝯ	28.j.v.	1 avril M 2J 31a	de Sevres 1811. V.D.
Bivouac	28.1	117.8	10 DC	28.j.v.	M or 1 avril 15av 31a	de Sevres 1811. V.D.
Tombeaux Musulmans en bríque	23.1		9 DC	28.j.v.	1 avril M 2Jl 31a	de Sevres 1811. V.D.
Vue des ruines d'Ombos	75.2	129.8	9 ꝯ	28.j.v.	1 avril M 2 Jn	de Sevres 1811. V.D.
Vue de Zaoùyéh	27.2	117.9	9 DC	28.j.v.	M 1 avril 15 av	de Sevres 1811. V.D.
Vue des ruines de Chnubis	75.3	119.21 &22	9 DC	28.j.v.	1 a M 2 Jn	de Sevres 1811. V.D.
Vue pittoresque du village de Qouss et du monument que l'on voit au milieu de la place.	80.3	129.1	9 DC	28.j.v.	M or 1 avril 15av	de Sevres 1811.
Embrasemènt de Salmie	28.2	119.1, 2&3	9 DC	28.j.v.	M. or 1 avril 15 av 31a	de Sevres 1811. V.D.

PLATES Title	after Denon pl.	border pl.	MARKS: incised	in green	in gold	in red (on most items the legend 'M.Imple' has been erased)
Vue de Boulac	23.2	119.14, 17&24	*9 ꓹ*	28.j.v.	1 avril M 2 Jn	de Sevres 1811. V.D.
Statues dites de Memnon	44.1	117.7	*9 ꓹ*	28.j.v.	M or 1 avril 15 av 31 av	de Sevres 1811. V.D.
Cimetière des Mamlouks à l'Est du Caire	23.2	119.13	*10 DL*	28.j.v.	1 avril M 2 Jn	de Sevres 1811. V.D.
La Fête dans le Harem	112.1	131.1 & 131.3	*9 ꓹ*	10. α	18 J	de Sevres 1811. V.D.
Autre Vue d'un Temple d'Hermontis	51.3	122.2	*10 ꓹ*	28.j.v.	6 aou 60 18^c	de Sevres 1811.
Le Memnonium	45.1	131.1	*8 DC*	10. α	aou	de Sevres 1811.
Vue de l'isle de Philoé de l'est à l'ouest	71.1	131.1	*9 S*	28.j.v.		de Sevres 1811.
Vue de l'intérieur de la Mosquée de St. Athanase	9.2	122.7	*10 ꓹ*	28.j.v.		de Sevres 1811.
Vue de l'Isle de Philoé	71.2	131.3	*9 DL*	24		de Sevres 1811.
Attaque d'arabes près les murs du Caire	24.2	131.3	*8 DC*	10. α	18 Jn	de Sevres 1811.
Temple d'Hermontis	51.1	131.1	*9 DC*	24	6 ao	de Sevres 1811.
Palais et Temples de Thêbes à Medynet-à-bou	45.2	131.1	*9 ꓹ*	24	30 avril	de Sevres 1811.
Fours Egyptiens	79.1		*oz ꓹ*	15.j.11.	30^{18v} 16 7bre	de Sevres 1812. V.D.
Vue de Zaòuyèh	25.1	123.4	*7 LD*	8j	Bo 3A 31 avril 30 8r	de Sevres 1812. V.D.
Arbre auquel on fait des offrandes	25.2	123.6	*8 DC*	10. α	Bou 3Ao 31 aout 30 18n	de Sevres 1812. V.D.
Jardin de l'institut du Caire	25.3	131.1	*9 DC*	10.	30^{18B} 3 aou	de Sevres 1812. V.D.

PLATES Title	after Denon pl.	border pl.	MARKS: incised	in green	in gold	in red (on most items the legend 'M.Imple' has been erased)
Tombeau Egyptien à Lycopolis	33.2	134.3, 4&5	OZ ꝛ	15.j.11	16 m ai....	de Sevres 1812. V.D.
Ruines du Termple d'Hermopolis	33.1	122.6	IO CC	15.j.11	16 m 30	de Sevres 1812. V.D.
Le Memnonium à Thêbes	42.5		IO ꝛ	15.j.11.	M 30 oct. 16 m $30^{18\,B}$	de Sevres 1812. V.D.
Pyramide d'Ellahoun	26.1	127.10	OZ ꝛ	15.j.11.	30^{18}w 16 m	de Sevres 1812. V.D.
Pyramide à Méidoùin	26.3	118.8	OZ ꝛ	15.j.11	16 6 fv	de Sevres 1812. V.D.
Vue de Siut ou Osiot	30.2	127.14	OZ ꝛ	15.j.1	30^{18}B 16 m N	de Sevres 18... V.D.
Sépultures arabes à Zaoye	30.3	122.12	IO DC	15.j.11	Mo 30^{oct} 16m 30^{iov}	de Sevres 1812. V.D.
Vue de Benisuéf	30.1	114.33 &116	OZ ꝛ	15.j.11	16m $V8^{re}$	de Sevres 1812. V.D.
Ruines d'un des Temples de l'isle d'Elephantine	66.3	132.1 126.3	IO DC	15.j.11		de Sevres 1812. V.D.
La dernière Pyramide en Remontant le Nil	62.2	119.4	OZ ꝛ	15.j.11		de Sevres 18... V.D.
Temple de Tentyris	38.2		OZ DL	15.j.11		de Sevres 18... V.D.
Temple de Tentyris	38.3	131.1 &130	IO DC ✳	15.j.11	M 30^{oct} 30^{18B}	de Sevres 1812. V.D.
Temple de Tentyris	38.4	135.23	OZ DL	15.j.11	30^{8}	de Sevres 18... V.D.
Temple de Tentyris	38.5		OZ ꝛ	15.j.11	M 30 8bre	V.D. V.D.
Ruines de la Porte d'un Temple d'Elephantine	65.1	123.1	IO DC	15.j.11	M 30 8bre 26 fv	de Sevres 18... V.D.
Carriere de Granite	68.2	119.19	II M		M 30 8bre 24 fv	de Sevres 18... V.D.
Ruines des Temples d'Elephantine	65.2	116.7	& ꝛ	15.j.11	M Oc.bre 6 fv	de Sevres 18... V.D.

PLATES *Title*		after Denon pl.	border pl.	MARKS: incised	in green	in gold	in red (on most items the legend 'M.Imple' has been erased)
Assiettes à monter	(1)	122.7		OZ DL	15.j.11	6 fv 16 7bre c.c. 16 7bre	de Sevres 1811.
	(2)	122.7		OZ J	15.j.11	6 fv 16 7bre c.c. 7bre 16	de Sevres 1811.
	(3)	122.7		9 DC	24	6fv 16	de Sevres 1811.
	(4)	122.7		OZ DL	15.j.11	6fv 14 8bre	de Sevres 1811.
	(5)	122.7		9 DC	10	6fv 16 7bre c.c. 16 7bre	de Sevres 1811.
	(6)	122.7		10 CC	15.j.11	6fv 14 8bre	de Sevres 1811.
	(7)	122.2		8 DC	15.j.11	30 8bre	de Sevres 1811.
	(8)	122.2		OZ CC	15.j.11	16 7bre c.c 16 7b	de Sevres 1811.
	(9)	122.2		10 DC	15.j.11	30 8b	de Sevres 1811.
	(10)	122.2		OZ J	15.j.11	30 8bre c.c.	de Sevres 1811.
	(11)	122.2		OZ J	15.j.11	6 fv 30 8b	de Sevres 1811.
	(12)	122.2			15.j.11		de Sevres 1811.
Compotiers	(1)	130		7LD		M. 2 Jet .....xt	de Sevres 1811. V.D.
	(2)	130		eleve 2 ligue H	24	M 2 jet . 6 . xt	de Sevres 1811.
	(3)	130		10 DL	25 ot	M.2.Jt .6. at	de Sevres 1811. V.D.
	(4)	130		7 LD		M.2.Jet 6. at	de Sevres 1811. V.D.
	(5)	130		7DL		(erased)	de Sevres 1811. V.D.
	(6)	130		7LD		M. 2 Jet 6. at	de Sevres 1811. V.D.
	(7)	130		7LD	24	M 2 Jet ... at	de Sevres 1811. V.D.
	(8)	130		7 LD		M.2 Jet 6 at	de Sevres 1811. V.D.

PLATES Title	after Denon pl.	border pl.	MARKS: incised	in green	in gold	in red (on most items the legend 'M.Imple' has been erased)
	(9) 130		7 ᴌD		M 2 Jet 6 at	de Sevres 1811. V.D.
	(10) 130		7 ᴌD	24	M 2 Jet 6 at	de Sevres 1811. V.D.
	(11) 130		10 Dᴌ	25 ot	M 2 Jet 6 at	de Sevres 1811. V.D.
	(12) 130		7ᴌD	24	M 2 Jet 6 at	de Sevres 1811. V.D.
Glacières (1)	133.1					
	133.3	Lining				
	116.6	Base	S a g Egyptien		M 6 at	de Sevres 1811.
		Body	(broad arrow) ↑	25 ot	30^{ocbre} M	M Imple de Sevres 1811.
		Lid	↑	24 jv	30^{8bre} M	
(2)	134.14-21					
	134.6-9	Lining				
	116.6	Base	S a g Egyptien		M 6 at	de Sevres 1811.
		Body				
		Lid	7		30^{8bre}	
Sucriers (1)	115.24		ᴌ Bo[12]	(erased)		de Sevres 1811.
(2)	115.24		10 dᴌ[13] Bo	24	M...6 at	de Sevres 1811.
Confituriers (1)	115.1			28.j...	M 16 7bre	M.Imple. de Sevres 1811./
(2)	115.1			28.j.v.	p.LM 16 7bre	M.Imple.de Sevres 1811.
Corbeilles (1)	59.7	Base	9			
		Basket	9 gn[14]			

PLATES Title	after Denon pl.	border pl.	MARKS: incised	in green	in gold	in red (on most items the legend 'M.Imple' has been erased)
(2)	59.7		Base **3**			de Sevres 1812
			Basket **ch** [15]			M.Imple.de Sevres 1812.
Figures (1)	135.32		All stamped SEVRES on front base			
(2)			.og. A.B. 28. jn. 10. No.1.			
(3)			.og.A.B.28. jn. 10. No.2.			
(4)			.og.A.B.4.Jn.d2			
			.og.A.B.4.jn.d2 a.li			
Vasques (1)	135.32		7	19.f.12	M 7 Avril	
(2)	135.32		10	24		

FOOTNOTES

1. Mark for 1810. See Bernard Chevallier, 'Les Marques en creux de la procelaine de Sevres' *Keramik-Freunde der Schweiz*, Mitteilungsblat, No 94 December 1980,p7
2. Mark of Joseph Thion (Thion père). Chevallier op.cit.p.22
3. Mark of Louis-Charles Descoins. Chevallier op.cit.p.13
4. Mark of Silvain Dupin. Chevallier op.cit.p.14
5. Mark for 1810. Chevallier op.cit.p.7
6. Mark for 1808. Chevallier loc.cit.
7. Probably the mark for 1807. Chevallier loc.cit.
8. Mark of Louis-Balthazard-Henry Davignon. Chevallier op.cit.p.12
9. Mark for 1811 (*onze*). Chevallier, op.cit.p.7.
10. A variation of the mark of L.-B.-H. Davignon. Chevallier op.cit.p.12
11. Mark of Claude-François-Loucet Choulet. Chevallier op. cit.p.11
12. Probably the mark of Martin Bougon
13. Mark of Louis-Mathias Chanou. Chevallier, op.cit.p.10
14. Mark of Charles Godin (Godin père). Chevallier op.cit.p.14
15. Mark of L.M. Chanou. Chevallier, op.cit.p.10
16. Mark of Jean-Jacques Oger. Chevallier, op.cit.p.20
17. Mark of approval used by Alexander Brongniart. Chevallier, op.cit.p.9
18. Mark for 1812. Chevallier, op.cit.p.7
19. Mark of Auguste-Marie Liance. Chevallier, op.cit.p.17

APPENDIX TWO

Dimensions

The Surtout: Maximum length: 6.641 metres
Maximum width: 0.76 metres
Maximum height: 0.76 metres

Central temple:	H. 48.3 cm
	W. 88.9 cm
	D. 69.2 cm
Smaller temples:	H. 23.3 cm
	W. 47.8 cm
	D. 25.8 cm
Pylons	H. 41.4 cm
	W. 65.3 cm
	D. 15.3 cm
Colonnades	H. 17.2 cm
	W. 5.6 cm
	L. 110.3 cm
Figures and sacred rams	H. 24.2 cm
	W. 9.7 cm
	L. 87.3 cm
Obelisks	H. 68.5 cm
	W. 10.8 cm
	D. 10.8 cm
Five bases	H. 7.5 cm
	W. 76 cm
	L. 99.4 cm
Two bases	H. 7.5 cm
	W. 46.2 cm
	L. 87.8 cm

The service:

Figures with bowls	H. 54 cm	
	Diam of bowl 26.9 cm	
	Width of figure 25.5 cm	
Sucriers	H. 32.4 cm	
	W. 11.8 cm	
	D. 18.5 cm	
Corbeilles	H. 24.9 cm	
	Diam 31.4 cm	
Seaux à glace	H. 23.1 cm	
	W. 26 cm	
	D. 19.4 cm	
Confituriers	H. 11.1 cm	
	W. 21.1 cm	
	D. 8.2 cm	
Compotiers	H. 6.6 cm	
	Diam. 24.2 cm	
Plates	Diam. 24 cm	Dimensions of the plates varies slightly
	H. 3 cm	for each example.

APPENDIX THREE

Conservation of the centrepiece
by Sue Service and Rupert Harris

When the service was acquired by the Museum much of it, in particular the centrepiece, was in a poor state. Damp and dirty storage conditions and the several major journeys it had been subjected to, together with general deterioration through use, had resulted in corrosion of the iron armatures and of the metal bases, and staining, chipping and cracking of the porcelain. The plaster fillings in the joints between sections of porcelain were crumbling and stained.

In order to restore the centrepiece to its original condition and to prevent further damage occurring, it was evident that each section would have to be disassembled, the porcelain cleaned and the bases treated, and then the whole reassembled on a new armature, the old iron rods and many of the nuts and washers being corroded beyond re-use. Dismantling the centrepiece would also provide an opportunity for detailed examination of the methods and materials used in its construction.

Removal of the nuts under the bases allowed the porcelain elements to be dismantled with some removal of the plaster fillings where these still bonded pieces together. Where the iron rods were cemented into the porcelain two different materials had been used as cements. Most widespread was the use of shellac which was brittle and easily removed. However, in some cases where extra strength had been required molten sulphur had been used. This had to be disolved out using carbon disulphide, a highly toxic and inflammable substance requiring extremely careful handling.

Due to its firing temperature, biscuit porcelain is very hard and has a low porosity. For this reason most of the staining was superficial and washing with warm water and a non-ionic detergent, followed by the use of a mildly

abrasive paste, removed most staining without damage to the porcelain. Iron stains caused by the armature were removed using material containing phosphoric acid. Some areas, notably the tops of the small temples still remained slightly mottled but it was felt that this was due to irregularities in the biscuit mixture.

Some of the rams had been badly broken in the past and repaired with shellac which had left brown smudges around the break edges. They were taken apart using hot water and the shellac cleaned off the edges with methylated spirits.

All broken pieces were bonded together with an epoxy resin adhesive and chips filled with a putty made up with epoxy resin, titanium dioxide and barium sulphate. Retouching of these areas was done with a clear lacquer mixed with pigments and matting agent to reproduce the appearance of the porcelain.

Examination of the metal bases showed that they were constructed from tinned black iron plate coated with a calcium carbonate gesso, overpainted with coloured stippled paint and two heavy coats of copal varnish. During the plateau's storage in damp conditions defects in the tin plate and in the paint surface allowed the penetration of moisture, resulting in heavy corrosion of the ironplate. However, most of the paint was still in place over the corroded metal although heavily pustulated in many places.

Relaying the paint on areas where lifting had begun was not possible, so this paint was also removed. Chemically spot treating the exposed rust presented the possibility of futher damaging the paintwork, most of the proprietory rust removers were not suitable. After many tests a rust convertor and inhibitor was found which met the necessary conditions.

On all the bases there was a good deal of untreated rust beneath the sensitive but intact paint, which was left untreated as no method could be found to effect a cure. Conservation was further complicated as the varnish layer over the paint had yellowed, changing considerably the original colour of the bases. With a view to rectifying the colour change solvent tests were made on the imitation porphyry bases to which the porcelain was attached. As is often the case, the varnish had become with age particularly difficult to dissolve. As a result it was decided to leave the varnish on these.

The same tests were then run on the seven lower bases. With these, probably due to a different varnish composition, tests were successful and the varnish was removed without damaging the paint underneath. Removal of the varnish changed the colour from what had been a dark shade of green to the original dark grey, black and white stippled finish.

After this treatment and the conversion of the exposed rusted areas to a stable state, repainting those areas of missing paint was possible. This was done using modern acrylic paints, each area being hand stippled with a fine brush.

Finally, each section of the plateau was revarnished regardless of whether the original varnish had been removed or not. This was done to seal as far as possible the iron plate from futher atmospheric attack.

In reconstructing the centrepiece some materials used differed from the originals as they were felt to be more suitable, bearing in mind the long term conservation of the object. The iron armature was replaced with stainless steel and the sulphur with epoxy putty, which although equally strong and durable is more easily and more safely reversed. Where shellac had been used as a cement for the rods, Polyfilla mixed with polyvinyl acetate emulsion was employed, and Polyfilla was also used to replace plaster as a filling, being stronger and more durable.